# Diet recommendations during TCM - Lung - Wind Heat affects the Lung

Please check these recommendations always with a nutrition consultant, therapist, doctor or dietician. The recipes and the list of ingredients are supporting the conventional medical therapy. The calorie disclosures of fresh ingredients (fruit and vegetables) vary according to quality and time of harvest. The contents were checked by a dietician and a nutrition consultant for the Traditional Chinese Medicine (TCM).

Author:
©2020 Josef Miligui
www.ebns.at

Source:
The lists are created from the EBNS database for nutritional counseling. The database is used by dietitians, therapists and doctors for advising the patient / client.

Literature:
The specialist literature and the training documents of the German and Austrian dietary and traditional Chinese medicine serve as a knowledge base. We have used the documents as a basis of knowledge, adapted it to our experience and completed them.
http://nutribook.info/

Production and publishing:
BoD – Books on Demand, Norderstedt
ISBN: 9783750414204

# Diet recommendations for TCM - Lung - Wind-heat affects the Lung

# 1 Treatment strategy

Drain (open surface and expel heat), cool heat, strengthen lungs Qi.

# 2 Avoid

Bitter or dehydrating food and drink, hot food and spices, smoked, fried, fat, grilled, sour food, tropical fruits, chicken, eggs, crustaceans, chives, dairy products, sweets, soft drinks.

# 3 Recipes

(rec.) = You can use more.
(little) = You should use less than specified
(omit) = omit.

## 3.1 8 treasures of rice

Strengthens kidney and bladder, builds up Qi, strengthens the spleen, repels moisture, reduces internal heat, prevents cancer, builds heart, calms nerves.
Cooking time approx. 1 hour
Calories p. portion: 212
4 portions

### Quantity of ingredients

Lily bulbs 1 table spoon / 5g. () - cool - sweet, bitter ........................................*
Longane 1 table spoon / 5g. () - warm - sweet......................................................*
King Solomon's-seal 1 table spoon / 5g. () - neutral - sweet, bitter...................*
Yam root, yam root tuber 1 table spoon / 5g. () - neutral - sweet......................*
Coix (seeds) YiYi Ren 1 table spoon / 5g. (yes) - cool - sweet, neutral ............*
Rice wild (nature rice) 1 1/2 cups / 240g. (yes) - neutral - sweet, bitter .... metal
Water 8-10 cups / 800g. (yes) - cool - salty................................................ earth

### Cooking instructions:

Each one 1 tbsp: Bai He, Longan, Yu Zhu, Da Zao, Shan Yao, Lian Mi, Yi Yi Ren, Qian Shi
Add hot water and soak for about 30 minutes. Then add 1 - 2 cups of rice (normal) and simmer for 1/2 to 1 hour until the rice is very soft. Or: Cook for about 3 hours with the herbs a congee. Then the herbs do not have to be soaked.

## 3.2  Basic recipe for a reissue soup (Congee)

Warms the stomach and spleen, harmonizes the intestine, forces Qi, reduces moisture.
Cooking time approx. 2-4 hours
Calories p. portion: 140
3 portions

### Quantity of ingredients
Rice variety any 1 cup / 120g. (rec.) - warm - sweet ................................. metal
Water 6 cups / 700g. (yes) - cool - salty ..................................................... earth

### Cooking instructions:
Cook rice and water in a ratio of about 1: 6. The amount of water determines the thickness of the mash (matter of taste).
Put the rice in a saucepan with a heavy lid. It is important to simmer the rice after a short boil on the slightest flame, otherwise it burns.
Boil the rice for 2-4 hours. The longer he cooks, the more he strengthens.
If you want to eat the dish for breakfast, you can put the rice on just before bedtime.
To be on the safe side, you should first check the behavior of your pot and cooker under observation for a similar amount of time, so that nothing burns.
Refrigerate for later use.

## 3.3  Celery juice

Strengthens stomach Qi, moisturizes, relaxes, builds up Qi, spreads.
Cooking time approx. 5 min
Calories p. portion: 33
1 portions
Allergens: L

### Quantity of ingredients
Celery root 1/2 piece / 200g. (rec.) - cool - sweet ...................................... earth
Water 1 cup / 120g. (yes) - cool - salty ....................................................... earth
Salt 1 pinch / 0,5g. (little) - cold - salty ...................................................... water

### Cooking instructions:
Peel celeriac and cut into pieces and juice. Mix with water and salt as needed.

## 3.4 Pear compote

Moisturizes lungs, reduces lung mucus, nourishes lungs Qi.
Cooking time approx. 20 min
Calories p. portion: 100
3 portions

### Quantity of ingredients
Water 1 1/2 cups / 240g. (yes) - cool - salty ............................................... earth
Pear 4 / 500g. (rec.) - cool - sweet, sour ..................................................... earth

### Cooking instructions:
Halve organic pears. Cores and skin can be used. Pear in the pot and add water. Simmer for up to 20 minutes until pears are tender.

## 3.5 Pear juice

Moisturizes lungs, reduces lung mucus, nourishes lungs Qi.
Cooking time approx. 5 min
Calories p. portion: 180
2 portions

### Quantity of ingredients
Pear 3 pieces / 600g. (rec.) - cool - sweet, sour .......................................... earth

### Cooking instructions:
Peel pears thinly (vitamins under the skin) and core. Juice in the juicer.

## 3.6 Radishjuice

Nourishes the lungs and spleen, distributes mucus, Dissolves mucus, dissolves stagnation, directs upwards.
Cooking time approx. 10 min
Calories p. portion: 9
1 portions

### Quantity of ingredients
Radish (white, green, purple-red) 1/2 piece / 50g. (rec.) - cool - sweet, acrid .......... metal
Water 1 cup / 120g. (yes) - cool - salty ...................................................................... earth

**Cooking instructions:**
Make the radish juice with the juicer or buy it at the food store.
The fresh press juice is extracted from the root.
For healing purposes one prefers the black radish because of its sharpness.
The pungent taste is due to the mustard oils in the radish juice.
They stimulate bile-juice production in the liver. This has two different effects in our body. The appetite and digestion are promoted and alleviates bile and liver disease.
Drink in small sips.

## 3.7 Rice congee with honey pear and black sesame

Especially good in kidney Yin deficiency, moisturizes lungs, cools heat, reduces lung mucus, produces humors, moisturizes, relaxes, builds up Qi, spreads, moisturizes intestines, nourishes Yin.
Cooking time approx. 10 min - 3 hours
Calories p. portion: 158
2 portions
Allergens: N

**Quantity of ingredients**
Basic recipe for a rice soup (Congee) 1 1/2 cups / 240g. (little) - neutral - sweet ...........*
Pear 2 pieces / 300g. (rec.) - cool - sweet, sour ........................................................ earth

**Cooking instructions:**
Cook rice congee according to basic recipe.
Fill pot with 3 cm of water and heat till it boils. Quarter the pears (with the skin and seeds) and simmer them covered with black sesame for 10 minutes. Mix with the rice.

## 3.8 Rice porridge with orange peel

Warms the stomach and spleen, harmonizes the intestine, forces Qi, reduces moisture. brings the Liver Qi in motion, cools heat, moisturizes, relaxes, builds up Qi, spreads. nourishes blood, moisturizes, relaxes, builds up Qi, spreads.
Cooking time approx. 10 min
Calories p. portion: 120
4 portions
Allergens: L

## Quantity of ingredients

Rice variety any 1 cup / 100g. (rec.) - warm - sweet ................................. metal
Water 6 cups / 600g. (yes) - cool - salty .................................................... earth
Olive oil 1 table spoon / 10g. (yes) - cool - sweet ...................................... earth
Champignon 1/2 cup / 50g. (rec.) - cool - sweet ........................................ earth
Celery sticks 1/2 bunch / 60g. (yes) - cool - sweet .................................... earth
Basic recipe for a chicken soup 3-4 table spoons / 40g. () - warm - * ............... *
Salt 1 pinch / 0,5g. (little) - cold - salty ...................................................... water

## Cooking instructions:

The day before boil the rice with the orange peel and water in a ratio of about 1: 6. The amount of water determines the thickness of the mash (pure matter of taste). Put the rice in a saucepan with good insulation and a heavy lid. It is important to simmer the rice after a short boil on the slightest flame, otherwise it burns. Boil the rice for 2-4 hours. The longer he cooks, the more he strengthens.

Heat the oil in a saucepan, add the chopped champignon and celery and sauté briefly. Add the rice. Add vegetable broth or water, warm up, salt.

## 3.9   Rice porridge with shrubs (seeds) Yi Yi Ren

Warms stomach, harmonizes the intestine, forces Qi, reduces moisture, forces spleen, nourishes and forces Lunge, reduces internal heat, moves Qi and blood, diuretic, cools in internal heat.
Cooking time approx. 25 min
Calories p. portion: 212
2 portions

## Quantity of ingredients

Water 4 cups / 450g. (yes) - cool - salty .................................................... earth
Rice variety any 1 cup / 120g. (rec.) - warm - sweet ................................. metal
Lemon peel 1/4 piece / 2g. () - cool - bitter ..................................................... fire
Coix (seeds) YiYi Ren 1/2 cup / 50g. (yes) - cool - sweet, neutral .................... *
Cress 1 table spoon / 6g. (rec.) - cool - sweet ............................................. metal

## Cooking instructions:

Cook rice porridge according to basic recipe with a half cup of Yi Yi Ren and lemon peel. Simmer for 1 hour and then sprinkle cress over it.
Tae from Dandelionroots
Cools liver fire, reduces internal heat, softens knots.
Cooking time approx. 15 min
Calories p. portion: 1
2 portions

**Quantity of ingredients**
Dandelion (young plants) 2-4 teaspoons / 6g. (rec.) - cool - sweet, bitter..... fire
Water 2 cup / 500g. (yes) - cool - salty....................................................... earth

**Cooking instructions:**
The chopped dandelion is doused with cold water. Heat the whole thing until it boils and cook for a minute. Then let it rest for ten minutes, filter and enjoy ... Sweet to taste with honey.

## 3.10 Tea from lime blossom

Reduces wind-heat and wind-coldness of the lungs.
Cooking time approx. 10 min
Calories p. portion: 0
2 portions
Allergens:
Quantity of ingredients
Water 2 cup / 500g. (yes) - cool - salty........................................... earth
Lime blossom tea 2 teaspoon  ............................................................. *

**Cooking instructions:**
Heat the water till it boils and put it aside. Add the linden blossoms and leave for 10 min. to let go. Sweet to taste with honey. Strain when pouring.

# 4   Effects of food

## 4.1   Use ingredients: recommendable

Barley
Barley malt
Cantaloupe
Celery root
Champignon
Chinese cabbage
Cress
Dandelion (young plants)
Elderberry blossom tee
Kohlrabi
Lime blossom tea
Mung bean sprouting
Oyster mushroom
Parsley root

Parsnip
Pear
Peppermint
Radish (white, green, purple-red)
Reishi mushroom
Rice (whole grain)
Rice flour
Rice long grain rice
Rice variety any
Shiitake, dried
Soybeans, black
Turmeric (yellow root)
Watermelon

## 4.2   Use ingredients: yes

Agar agar (kelp)
Apple (sweet)
Apple juice (natural cloudy)
Arrowroot
Artichoke
Avocado
Beer (Pils)
Bitter melon
Breadcrumbs (wheat bread, bread roll)
Broad beans (thick beans)
Burdock root tea
Calamari
Celery sticks
Chard
Chlorella (fresh water)
Coix (seeds) YiYi Ren
Cucumber
Dandelionroots tea
Grape juice red
Grape juice white
Grapes red
Herbs various
Honey
Kombu seaweed (Saccharina japonica)
Malt
Miso paste (soy bean paste)
Morel (black, dried)
Multi-grain bread (gray bread)
Mung bean
Olive oil
Olives
Peas

Peas, green
Potato
Pumpkin seeds
Radish
Radish black
Red cabbage
Rice black
Rice noodles
Rice red
Rice round grain
Rice sweet
Rice wild (nature rice)
Rye
Rye flour
Salsify
Soy sauce
Soybean milk
Soybeans, yellow
Sweet potato
Thyme
Vanilla
Vanilla powder
Vegetable juice
Wakame
Water
Water hot
Wheat flour
Wheat germ oil
White beans
White bread (wheat bread)
Yarrow tea
Zucchini

## 4.3   Use ingredients: little

Anise (Common Fennel)
Asparagus (green or white)
Aubergine
Bamboo shoots
Basic recipe for a rice soup (Congee)
Basic recipe for a vegetable soup
(nutritious)
Beef meat (calf)
Blueberry juice
Broccoli
Butter organic
Cashews
Cauliflower
Chickpeas
Coconut flakes
Coconut grated

Coriander
Cumin (Caraway seed)
Deer meat
Dill
Ground
Ground caraway
Lentils black
Lentils red
Maple syrup
Marjoram
Millet
Millet flakes
Mustard seeds
Onion read
Onion white
Peanuts

Pear juice
Pepper Cayenne
Pepper white (ground)
Peppercorns
Pheasant
Raspberry dried (immature)
Rice Basmati
Salt
Sour milk cheese 20%
Soy Tofu

Spinach
Star anise
Tarragon (Estragon)
Trout
Wheat
Wheat bulgur
Wheat flakes
Wheat semolina
Wheat semolina for children

## 4.4   Do not use contra-acting foods

Adzuki beans
Almond marzipan
Almond milk
Almond puree
Amaranth
Anchovy / Sardine
Apple (sour)
Apricot
Apricots
Balm
Banana
Banana (cooking banana)
Basil
Basil (fresh)
Bean oil
Beef fillet
Beef liver
Beef meat
Beef meatbones
Beef stomach
Beer (Top-fermented German dark beer)
Black tea
Blackberry´s
Black-eyed peas
Blueberry
Boxhorn clover seeds
Brussels sprouts
Buckwheat
Bulgur (cereals)
Buttermilk
Carambola (Star fruit)
Carp
Carrot
Carrot (Early Carrot)
Carrot juice without sugar
Caviar
Cereal coffee
Cherry
Cherry juice
Chestnuts

Chicken egg
Chicken liver
Chicken meat
Chicken stomach
Chicory
Chili (pod or ground)
Chives
Chocolate
Cinnamon ground
Cinnamon sticks
Clementines
Clove
Cocoa
Coconut milk
Cod
Coffee
Corn
Corn Grease (Polenta)
Couscous
Cow's milk (1.5% fat)
Cow's milk (whole milk 3.5% fat)
Crab
Cranberry
Cranberry juice
Cream, sweet 30%
Crucian
Curcuma
Curd cheese 20%
Curd cheese 40%
Currant (black)
Currant (red)
Currant (white)
Curry
Dates dried
Deer meat
Duck (heart)
Duck (slaughtered)
Eel
Endive salad
Fennel
Fennel tea

Feta cheese
Fig
Fig dried
Fish pieces mixed (fresh water)
French beans
Fresh cheese
Garlic
Ginger fresh
Ginger powder
Goat
Goat and sheep's milk
Goat cheese
Goose
Goose egg
Goose parts
Gooseberry
Gourd
Grapefruit (Pomelo)
Grapefruit juice
Grapes white
Grass carp
Green spelt
Green tea
Hawthorn
Hazelnuts
Herring
Hyssop
Iceberg lettuce
Juniper berry
Kefir
Kiwi
Kumquats
Lamb bones
Lamb meat
Lamb shoulder
Lamb's lettuce
Leek
Lemon
Lemon juice
Lentils
Lentils yellow
Lettuce
Lime
Lobster
Longane
Lovage
Lychee
Lychee in Preserved
Mallow (Malva sylvestris) blossom tea
Mango
Margarine
Margarine (diet)
Mold cheese
Mozzarella

Mulberry fruit
Mullet
Mussels
Mutton
Mutton
Nutmeg
Oat
Oat flakes (whole grain)
Oat flour
Oat fusion (baby food)
Oat meal
Octopus
Okra
Onion (shallot)
Onion (spring onion)
Orange
Orange juice
Oregano dried
Oysters
Papaya
Parmesan
Parsley
Peaches
Peaches (canned)
Peanut oil
Peppers
Peppers (rose peppers)
Perch
Pigeon
Pimento
Pine nuts
Pineapple
Pineapple (from a can)
Pineapple juice without sugar
Pistachios
Plaice
Plum
Pomegranate
Poppy
Pork heart
Pork knuckle
Pork liver
Pork meat
Pork skin
Pork stomach
Pumpkin
Pumpkin seed oil
Quail
Quail egg
Quince
Quinoa
Rabbit
Rabbit liver
Rabbit meat

Radicchio
Raisins
Rapeseed oil
Raspberry
Red wine
Rhubarb
Rice malt
Romaine lettuce / lettuce salad
Rose hip tea
Rosemary
Saffron
Sage
Sago (cereals)
Sake
Salmon
Sauerkraut (cutted cabbage fermented)
Seacrab
Sesame oil
Shark
Shrimp
Shrimps
Sorrel
Sour cherries
Sour cream 15% fat
Sour milk
Soybean oil
Spelled (Dark) bread
Spelled grain
Spelled semolina

Spelled wholemeal flour
Spiny lobsters
Spirit
Strawberries
Strawberry Juice
Sugar brown
Sugar candy white
Sugar cane sugar
Sugar fructose - fruit sugar
Sugar glucose - grapes sugar
Sugar Milk Sugar
Sugar molasses
Sugar white
Sunflower oil
Sunflower seeds
Tangerine
Tomato
Tuna
Turkey breast meat
Umeboshi plums (Japanese apricots)
Vinegar (Apple vinegar)
Walnuts
Wheat beer
Wheat bran
White wine
Wild boar meat
Yogi tea
Yogurt (natural, 1.5% fat)
Yogurt (natural, 3.5% fat)

# 5   Complementary

## 5.1   Barberry roots

Berberis
Preparation: Healing tea (infusion)
Clears heat, dries moisture. Regulates liver-qi, clears lung-heat / mucus-heat, cools stomach fire.
Strengthens and strengthens the liver. Effective in liver disease, especially in jaundice and hepatitis. Immune System Stimulant, Digestive, removes protozoan parasites (amoebae), activates the thyroid gland and is considered to be one of the most beneficial herbs. One of the most effective herbs for correcting spleen, gall bladder and liver function, it is also effective against jaundice, gastritis, liver and kidney blockage and weakness. An effective stomach and intestinal and blood cleanser. It helps to remove blockages and deposits. Because it has antiseptic properties, it helps with liver problems.
Do not use in pregnancy.

## 5.2   Chamomile

Chamaemelum nobile
Preparation: Healing tea (infusion)
Regulates liver-Qi, triggers stagnation, lowers liver-yang and internal wind, regulates lung-qi, induces hot-mucus from the lungs, evokes wind-heat and moisture-heat. Cooling.
Pour 2 teaspoons of the tea into 250 ml of boiling water and leave for 10 minutes. Then sieve. Drink 2 to 3 cups per day as needed.
Active ingredients: Äth. Oil: chamazulen, bisabolol, flavonoids, coumarins
Continuous use is not recommended, otherwise harmless.

## 5.3   Coneflowers

Echinacea purpurea
Preparation: Decoction
Activates Wie-Qi, strengthens lung- and stomach-Qi.
Use: finished preparations
The well-known complementary doctor Dr. med. However, Keith Block attributed Essiac only a weak antitumor effect and suggested that the healing results of the tea around the turn of the century may have been a lot better because of the significantly lower levels of stress on people with carcinogenic substances.

## 5.4   Elderberry (flowers)

Sambucus nigra
Preparation: Decoction
Relieves wind-cold and wind-heat, soothes Shen.
Add 2 - 3 teaspoons of dried flowers to 150 ml of boiling water, cover for 3 - 5 min. Strain and drink as hot as possible. Drops that have collected in the lid into the tea, because here are also valuable ingredients.

## 5.5   Mint

Mentha arvensis
Preparation: Healing tea (infusion)
Eliminates internal heat, dispels wind-heat.
Pour 2-4 g with 250 ml of boiling water and let stand for 10 minutes. Then sieve. Drink in a single dose on an empty stomach.

Casting: Pour 1 g of powder with hot water, leave to simmer and then drink on an empty stomach, possibly sweeten the tea with a little honey; Ointment: mix some mint powder with yellow vaseline, almond oil, lanolin or other fat base; then apply the cooling and soothing ointment to the head, chest, abdomen or other hot, painful, jammed or inflamed parts of the body.
Do not use on: severe shivering, nervous exhaustion.

## 5.6   Peppermint

Menthae, Herba
Preparation: Healing tea (infusion)
Relieves the internal wind of the body, clears the head and eyes, detoxifies the skin. Moves and regulates qi, lowering stomach-qi. Clarifying wind-heat, detoxifying, moving.
Pour 2-10 g with 250 ml of boiling water and let stand for 10 minutes. Then sieve. Drink 2 to 3 cups per day as needed.
Active ingredients: essential oil (menthol), tannins, flavonoids, bitter substances
Do not cook for long; Do not use on: Biao-Xu sweating or pregnancy.

## 5.7   Plantain

Plantago lanceolata/major, herb.
Preparation: Healing tea (infusion)
Clears lung heat and dissipates heat-phlegm.
Plantain is one of the best herbs to break up the mucous deposits of the intestine. And he is one of the best blood cleaners. Plantain is a good liverwort and also improves the function of the kidneys. It helps prevent bloating and diarrhea. Overall, he is one of the largest medicinal herbs of nature. It tastes delicious in a salad (along with dandelion leaves) and probably grows in your own backyard.

## 5.8   Sage

Salvia
Preparation: Healing tea (infusion)
Expels Mucus, Dries, Guides Down, Activates Wei Qi, Strengthens Qi.
Äth. Oils containing many bitter substances and tannins should not be overdosed in order not to pollute the stomach.
Do not use on: Pregnancy

# 6 Basics of Nutrition

The basic principles of nutrition described herein are general recommendations. They are not aimed at a specific form of therapy. Recommendations concerning a therapy have priority.

## 6.1 Nutrition

Regular meals in a relaxed atmosphere. A warm breakfast is considered a good start into the day.

The main meals ought to be taken for lunch – supper in the early evening. Pay attention to feeling hungry or sated: don't eat too much nor remain hungry is the rule

Prepare the meals freshly from natural, regional products. Frozen, heat-conserved, industrially prepared or foodstuffs cooked in the microwave oven are rejected.

Choice of foodstuffs according to the season: more cooling food in summer, more warming food in winter.

Eat cooked food at least twice a day. Food and drinks ought to be lukewarm, never ice-cold or hot.

Raw vegetables, briefly cooked vegetables, freshly squeezed juices and mineral water are not recommended. Milk and dairy products are only included in the diet if they don't cause problems. Don't use therapeutic recipes over a longer period without consulting your doctor or therapist.

**Varied food**
Enjoy the diversity of foodstuffs. Characteristics of a balanced nutrition are variety, suitable combination and a balanced quantity of rich and low energy foodstuffs (on one hand avoiding undersupply with essential nutrients and on the other hand to take to many undesirable substances).

**A lot of Cereal Products - and Potatoes**
Bread, pasta, rice, cereal flakes (best wholemeal) as well as potatoes contain almost no fat, but many vitamins, mineral nutrients, trace elements, roughage and secondary plant substances. These foodstuffs ought to be taken with low-fat side dishes.

**Vegetables and Fruit – „Take Five" every day ...** 5 portions of vegetables and fruit a day, as fresh as possible, briefly cooked, or maybe one portion as a juice – ideal as a side dish to every meal as well as snack between meals: Thus a lot of vitamins, mineral nutrients as well as roughage and secondary plant substances

### Daily milk and dairy products
Milk and Dairy Products every Day, once or twice per Week Fish; meat, sausages as well as eggs moderately. These foodstuffs contain valuable nutrients like calcium in the milk, iodine selenium and omega-3 fat acids in saltwater fish. Meat is favorable due to its high content of disposable iron and the vitamins B1, B6 and B12. Quantities of 300 – 600 g meat and sausage per week are sufficient. Prefer low-fat products, especially in meat- and dairy products.

### Low-fat and fatty Foodstuffs
Fat supplies us with essential fat acids and fatty foodstuffs contain also fat-soluble vitamins. Fat is high in energy; therefore much fat in the food may cause overweight, possibly also cancer. Too many saturated fat acids may further a tendency for cardio-vascular diseases in the long term. Prefer vegetable oils and fats (e.g. rapeseed-, olive-, soya-oils and solid fats produced therefrom). Beware of invisible fat in meat- and dairy products, pastry and sweets as well as in fast-food and convenience foods. 70 – 90 g fat per day is sufficient.

### Moderately Sugar and Salt
Take sugar and foods/drinks containing various kinds of sugar (e.g. glucose syrup) only occasionally. Use herbs and spices as well as a little salt creatively. Prefer salt containing iodine.

### Plenty of Liquids
Water is absolutely essential. Drink 1-2 l liquids every day. Prefer water (with or without gas) and other low-calorie drinks. Alcoholic drinks should not be taken.

### Tasty Dishes, carefully cooked
Cook the meals with as low temperatures and as short as possible, using little water and fat – this preserves the original taste, keeps the nutrients intact and prevents the production of harmful compounds.

### Take time and enjoy the food
Take your Time and enjoy your Food
Eating consciously helps to eat right. The eye enjoys food, too. It's fun, invites to enjoy varied dishes and stimulates the feeling of satiety.

### Watch your Weight and stay in Motion
A balanced diet and a lot of exercise and sport (30 – 60 min/day) are a healthy combination. The right weight furthers well-being and health.

Thermals, directional effectiveness, digestive power
There are various criteria for judging the effectiveness of herbs and foodstuffs.
The use of certain herbs and ingredients is based on observations of the effects on the body which these foodstuffs, herbs and spices show after having eaten them. The medical science has developed following system: Every ingredient or herb has a directional effectiveness. Furthermore, there are herbs which have a special effect on certain organs.
The basic condition for a healthy metabolism is to obtain sufficient energy from food and that the digestive process doesn't use too much energy. An easily digestible meal makes content and sated, doesn't cause flatulence and fatigue after the meal. The perfect spices increase the healthiness of our meals. Very often, just small doses of herbs and spices will suffice. They are not used to make us sated, but to help our digestive organs to digest the food.

## 6.2   Recipes

The recipes list the ingredients to be used and the cooking instructions show how the dish is prepared. The list of ingredients shows the concerned quantities as well as the relevance for the therapy. If you find „omit", try to comply or find an alternative from the „list of recommended foodstuffs". Mostly it shall result just in a small change of taste when you simply avoid this ingredient.
Mild cooking methods: boiling, stewing, poaching, steaming
Strong cooking methods: barbecuing, roasting, frying, smoking
Balanced cooking methods: deep-frying, baking brick
Deep-freezing and warming in the microwave oven should be avoided (denaturalization).

## 6.3   Foodstuffs

Foodstuffs have an effect on body and soul like medicinal herbs, only a very much milder one. Dietary advice is mainly based on regional foodstuffs. The knowledge about the effects of each foodstuff and the knowledge, when which foodstuff shall be used, is based on the school medicine. Use ecologic-organic products, if possible. As everything should be cooked for a long time due to a better digestability and very rarely eaten raw, the food agrees with everyone.
The classification of the foodstuffs according to their effect on the body is the basis in order to achieve a harmonious status of health.
Dietary advisors do not recommend certain foodstuffs for everyone. The individual diet is tailor-made for the individual constitution.

Buy only fresh and ripe fruit and vegetables. You ought to leave unripe fruit and vegetables and such with brown spots and wilted leaves behind in the market. In this case take deep-frozen goods (never ready-to-serve dishes!). Fruit and vegetables are deep-frozen immediately after harvesting and often contain more vitamins and minerals than the goods from the vegetable shelf. Whereas conserved or tinned goods contain very much less biological substances. Also, salt, sugar and others are mostly added to the latter. Never leave the foodstuffs in the water after washing them to avoid that many vital substances get drowned. Clean salads, fruit and vegetables immediately before serving.

Please make sure of the hygienic processing of foodstuffs. Clean your salads, fruit and vegetables carefully. When cooking with meat, prepare all ingredients first and then process the meat products. Clean the worktop and tools very carefully. Wooden surfaces ought to be treated with a mild disinfectant regularly in order to reduce germination. Store fruit and vegetables separately, if possible. Harvested fruit and vegetables are still alive and emit e.g. ethylene gas, which makes other products ripen and age faster. Keep meat and fish in the closed packaging or store them in the fridge in closed containers.

## 6.4  Herbs

There are some basic rules for storing medicinal herbs. On principle, herbs must be protected from direct sunlight, humidity and heat.

Containers for the storage of herbs may be glasses, ceramic jars and even plastic containers. However, plastic is a rather unsuitable material and should only be a short-term solution. In case of glass containers, use a dark material.

Medicinal herbs cannot be kept for any long period. The shelf life of herbs is limited. However, it can be prolonged with suitable storage. The place should be dark, rather cool and absolutely dry. A wooden medicine cabinet, placed not directly next to a source of heat, would be ideal. Never buy large quantities of herbs so as not to have to throw them away. Label the container with the name of the herb and the date of harvesting or processing.

# 7   Other dietic-books

The following syndromes of dietetics, TCM or for a therapy supplement for cancer are available.

## Dietetics

E001. Nutrition of the infant - baby food
E002. Nutrition during lactation
E003. Nutrition in old age
E004. Nutrition of children and adolescents
E005. Nutrition of athletes
E006. Light weight
E007. Pregnancy
E008. Full food

**Protein and electrolyte - kidneys**
E009. (hemodialysis) dialysis treatment
E010. Acute renal failure
E011. Chronic renal insufficiency
E012. Nephrotic syndrome
E013. Kidney stones (nephrolithiasis)

**Gastrointestinal tract - pancreas**
E014. Acute pancreatitis (inflammation of the pancreas)
E015. Chronic pancreatitis (inflammation of the pancreas)

**Gastrointestinal tract - small intestine and large intestine**
E016. Acute obstipation (constipation)
E017. Chronic obstipation (constipation)
E018. Colon irritabile
E019. Diverticulitis
E020. Acquired lactose intolerance (lactose malabsorption)
E021. Fructose malabsorption
E022. Glutensensitive enteropathy (celiac disease)
E023. Colectomy
E024. Short Bowel Syndrome

**Gastrointestinal tract - liver, gallbladder, bile ducts**
E025. Acute and chronic hepatitis (inflammation of the liver)
E026. Cholelithiasis (bile stones)
E027. fatty liver
E028. cirrhosis

**Gastrointestinal tract - Stomach and duodenal intestine**
E029. Acute gastritis
E030. Chronic gastritis
E031. Stomach bleeding
E032. Ulcus ventriculi and duodenal ulcer
E033. Condition after gastric surgery

**Gastrointestinal tract - oral cavity and esophagus**
E034. Stomatitis
E035. Esophageal carcinoma (esophageal cancer)
E036. Refluosophagitis (heartburn)

**Special diseases**
E037. Phenylketonuria (PKU)
E038. Rheumatic joint diseases

**Metabolism**
E039. Obesity (overweight)
E040. Diabetes mellitus
E041. Eating disorders (underweight)

**Fat metabolism**
E042. Hypercholesterolaemia (increased cholesterol level)
E043. Hepatic Encephalopathy

**Heart and circulation**
E044. Arteriosclerosis (arterial calcification)
E045. Heart insufficiency
E046. Hypertension
E047. Hyperuricaemia and gout

**Changed nutrient requirements**
E048. In case of fever
E049. For malignant diseases
E050. After burns
E051. Radiation and chemotherapy

# CANCER
E100. Pancreatic cancer
E101. Bladder cancer
E102. Blood cancer (leukemia)
E103. Breast cancer
E104. Colorectal cancer
E105. Gastric cancer
E106. Kidney cancer
E107. Esophageal cancer

# TCM
E200. Bladder - moisture heat in the bladder
E201. Bladder - moisture and cold in the bladder
E202. Bladder - emptiness and cold in the bladder
E203. Large intestine - external cold affects the large intestine
E204. Large intestine - moisture heat in the large intestine
E205. Large intestine - heat blocks the intestine II acute
E206. Large intestine - dryness of the colon
E207. Large intestine - Yang deficiency (cold)
E208. Heart - Blood insufficiency
E209. Heart - Blood stagnation
E210. Heart - Fire
E211. Heart - Hot mucus clogs the heart pores

E212. Heart - Cold mucus clogs the heart pores
E213. Heart - Qi deficiency
E214. Heart - Yang deficiency
E215. Heart - Yin deficiency
E216. Liver - Ascending Liver Yang
E217. Liver - Blood deficiency
E218. Liver - Blood stagnation
E219. Liver - Moisture heat in liver and gall bladder
E220. Liver - Fire
E221. Liver - Gall bladder Qi-Empty
E222. Liver - Cold in the liver meridian
E223. Liver - Qi stagnation
E224. Liver - Wind
E225. Liver - Wind with ascending liver Yang
E226. Liver - Wind with blood anemic
E227. Liver - Wind with extreme heat
E228. Lung - Qi deficiency
E229. Lung - Mucus-moisture in the lungs
E230. Lung - Mucus-heat in the lungs
E231. Lung - Mucus-cold in the lungs
E232. Lung - Dryness of the lungs
E233. Lung - Wind-heat attacks the lungs
E234. Lung - Wind-cold affects the lungs
E235. Lung - Yin deficiency
E236. Stomach - Bloodstagnation
E237. Stomach - Fire
E238. Stomach - Cold with liquid
E239. Stomach - Nutrition stagnation
E240. Stomach - Qi deficiency
E241. Stomach - Rebellious Qi
E242. Stomach - Yin Emptiness
E243. Spleen - Heat and moisture attack the spleen
E244. Spleen - Coldness and moisture affects the spleen
E245. Spleen - Qi deficiency
E246. Spleen - Qi deficiency + Declining spleen Qi
E247. Spleen - Qi deficiency + spleen does not control the blood
E248. Spleen - Yang deficiency
E249. Kidney - Heart and kidney no longer communicate
E250. Kidney - Jing deficiency
E251. Kidney - Kidneys cannot receive the Qi
E252. Kidney - Qi is not stable
E253. Kidney - Yang deficiency
E254. Kidney - Yin deficiency


For further information visit nutribook.info.

# 8   EBNS - Software for nutritional counseling

The main task of the database is to create personalized nutritional advice for each patient individually. The database was developed for Dietetics and Traditional Chinese Medicine.

The Database supports training and advices in the daily work routine.

The computer program provides lists of recipes, ingredients and herbs, which are given to the client. individually adjustable according to patient's request from whole food to vegetarians (lacto, ovo, ...). For every register there is an information sheet which can be given to the client. All texts can be individually designed.

The syndromes can be combined and result in an intersection of the recommended recipes and ingredients. The automated diagnosis for the TCM enables you to check your experience during the training as well as to confirm your diagnosis in the working day. You select several predefined symptoms and have the program automatically display the relevant syndromes.

How to work with the database:
Select the patient / client, select one or more of the syndromes you diagnosed and print the folder.

You can change all values, create new symptoms or syndromes, develop recipes, change or adapt ingredients and herbs to your findings. In simple client management, all relevant data about the person is stored. You get an overview of the past diagnoses and the development of the course of the disease.

As a consultant you save a lot of time when you print out the recipe, food and herbal lists for the recognized syndromes and give them to the clients. You can use this time for a personal conversation. With the database, dieticians and nutritionists can view the nutrients and trace elements for each recipe and develop recipes for syndromes even with suggested ingredients.

All recipe and grocery lists can also be ordered from me as a combination of several diseases. I wish all readers good luck, health and happiness in life.
More information can be found at www.ebns.at.
Volunteer: www.krebsinfo.at
Josef Miligui